Contents

Some words are shown in bold, **like this**. You can find them in the picture glossary on page 23.

What is a living thing?

Living things are things that grow.

People, animals, and plants are living things.

Which things in the picture are living and which are not?

What is water?

Water is a **liquid**.

You can see through water. Water has no smell or taste.

All living things need water.

Why do we need water?

We need water to drink.

You need water to move, talk, think, and grow.

If we do not drink water, we get **thirsty** and feel ill.

Where does water come from?

clouds

rain

Water falls from clouds as rain.

Rain fills up rivers, lakes, and the sea.

Pipes bring clean water to our homes and gardens.

Do plants need water?

Plants need water to grow.

Fill a few pots with soil.

Plant a **seed** into each pot.

Water some pots every day but do not water the others.

Which seeds do you think will grow?

Where do plants get water from?

Most plants have **roots** under the soil.

The roots take in rain that falls onto the soil.

These plants have long roots in the water.

The roots take in the pond water.

Do animals need water?

Animals need to drink water too.

Some animals like to wash
with water!

Some animals find their food
in water.

This bird needs to live near water.

What needs a lot of water?

Some animals need to keep wet all the time.

This toad lives near a pond so it can keep wet.

These dolphins live in seawater all the time.

What needs little water?

Camels do not have to drink very often.

A camel can store water in its body.

Cactus plants do not need
much water.

They live in the **desert** where it
hardly ever rains.

Can you guess?

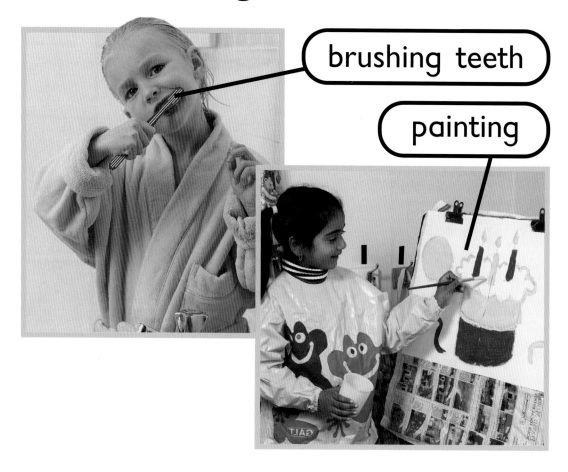

brushing teeth

painting

People must have water for drinking.

What else do people need water for?

Glossary

 **desert** a hot, dry, sandy place where it hardly ever rains

 **liquid** something runny that you can pour, like water or milk

 **roots** part of a plant that sucks up water

 **seed** a hard, ball-shaped part of a plant that grows into a new plant

 **thirsty** feeling as though you badly need a drink

Index

Note to parents and teachers

Reading non-fiction texts for information is an important part of a child's literacy development. Readers can be encouraged to ask simple questions and then use the text to find the answers. Most chapters in this book begin with a question. Read the questions together. Look at the pictures. Talk about what the answer might be. Then read the text to find out if your predictions were correct. To develop readers' enquiry skills, encourage them to think of other questions they might ask about the topic. Discuss where you could find the answers. Assist children in using the contents page, picture glossary and index to practise research skills and new vocabulary.